Prehistoric Britain

Bronze Age and Iron Age

Hill Forts

Dawn Finch

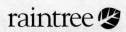

raintree

a Capstone company — publishers for children

Raintree is an imprint of Capstone Global Library Limited, a company incorporated in England and Wales having its registered office at 264 Banbury Road, Oxford, OX2 7DY – Registered company number: 6695582

www.raintree.co.uk
myorders@raintree.co.uk

Edited by Helen Cox Cannons
Designed by Philippa Jenkins
Original illustrations © Capstone Global Library Limited 2017
Illustrations Oxford Designers and Illustrators, Philippa Jenkins p10
Picture research by Kelli Lageson
Production by Steve Walker
Originated by Capstone Global Library Limited
Printed and bound in China

ISBN 978 1 4747 3046 4
21 20 19 18 17
10 9 8 7 6 5 4 3 2 1

British Library Cataloguing in Publication Data
A full catalogue record for this book is available from the British Library.

Acknowledgements
We would like to thank the following for permission to reproduce photographs: Alamy Stock Photo: geogphoto, 16, Robert Morris, 20 (bottom), Steve Speller 19, Skyscan Photolibrary, cover; Bennachie Centre/Dawn Finch: 9, 12, 26 (bottom), 27 (top and bottom); Bridgeman Images: Karen Guffogg, 21 (bottom), Paul Birkbeck, 28; Capstone: 5, 18 (top), 20 (top), 22 (top), 24 (top), 26 (top); Dawn Finch: 21 (top), 24 (bottom), 25; Dreamstime: Hel080808, 14 (bottom); Elgin Museum/Dawn Finch: 6, 7, 15; Reproduced by kind permission of English Heritage/Dawn Finch: 8, 13; Shutterstock: Claudio Divizia, 14 (top), 23, Helen Hotson, 11, Psychocy, 22 (bottom), singh_lens, design element (cover and throughout); SuperStock: Capture Ltd/LatitudeStock, 18 (bottom), Pantheon/Panth/ardea.com/Dae Saditorn, 4, robertharding, 17.

The author and publishers would like to thank Historic Scotland, Historic England and English Heritage. Thanks also goes to Mark Bowden, Senior Investigator and Team Manager at Historic England for his invaluable help in the preparation of this book. Also, thank you to Janet Trythall (Vice President of the Moray Society) and the curators and volunteers at Elgin Museum, Scotland, for all their help and for permission to view and photograph their collection.

Every effort has been made to contact copyright holders of material reproduced in this book. Any omissions will be rectified in subsequent printings if notice is given to the publisher. All the internet addresses (URLs) given in this book were valid at the time of going to press. However, due to the dynamic nature of the internet, some addresses may have changed, or sites may have changed or ceased to exist since publication. While the author and publisher regret any inconvenience this may cause readers, no responsibility for any such changes can be accepted by either the author or the publisher.

Contents

Some words in this book appear in bold, **like this.** You can find out what they mean by looking in the glossary.

What are hill forts?

Hill forts are walled places, or **enclosures**, made with high walls, fences and ditches. People built and lived in hill forts in the British Isles during periods we now know as the late **Neolithic** period, the Bronze Age and the Iron Age. The Bronze Age was a period of time from 2200 BC to 800 BC. It was followed by the Iron Age, which ended around AD 43, when the Romans invaded Britain.

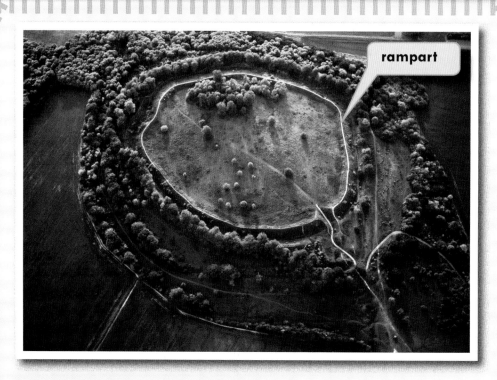

rampart

Building a picture

Archaeologists believe that there were many thousands of hill forts all over the British Isles. Today, there are over 3,000 hill forts remaining. Archaeologists have studied hill forts for over 150 years. At first archaeologists only looked at the **ramparts**. More recently they have looked for **evidence** of buildings and life within the ramparts.

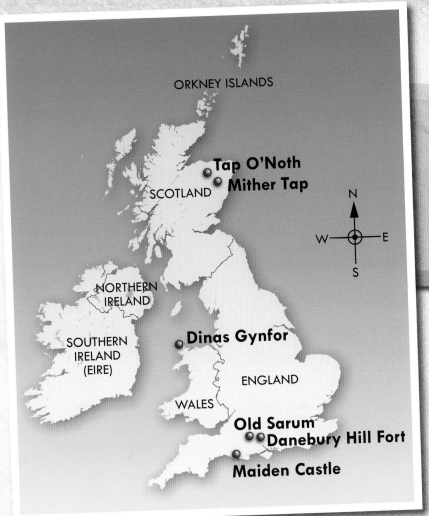

ORKNEY ISLANDS

Tap O'Noth
Mither Tap
SCOTLAND

N
W—E
S

NORTHERN
IRELAND

SOUTHERN
IRELAND
(EIRE)

Dinas Gynfor

ENGLAND

WALES

Old Sarum
Danebury Hill Fort

Maiden Castle

This map shows where the hill forts mentioned in this book are in the United Kingdom.

What are ramparts?

Hill forts were surrounded by ramparts. Ramparts were high banks made of earth and stone that were built around the edge of a fort. Sometimes there were many ramparts around a hill fort, with ditches in between each one. Ramparts may also have had wooden walkways around the top of them, and some had fences along the walkways to add even more protection.

Hill fort remains

The remains of Bronze Age and Iron Age hill forts can be found around the British Isles today. Some hill forts were built on high ground and hills, while some were built on the tops of cliffs beside the sea. This book looks at some of these sites and what life in a prehistoric hill fort was like.

Who built hill forts?

New metals

During the Bronze Age, the people of the British Isles began to make tools using metal instead of stone. Bronze Age people made a new metal – bronze. Bronze is made by taking two other metals, copper and tin, and melting them together.

On their own, copper and tin are too soft to make tools with, but they are strong when mixed together to make bronze. The people used this stronger metal for tools to help them build larger and better buildings. They also used it to work the land around them. In time, they began to use an even stronger metal – iron. Then the Bronze Age became the Iron Age.

This rock has had a shape carved into it so that softened metal could be hammered in to make an axe head.

Iron Age people became so good at using metal that they began to make beautiful things, like this brooch.

Iron Age tools and weapons

During the Iron Age, people used tools to clear the land to create bigger farms. They made things like axes, spears and arrowheads for better hunting and building. People began to work out how to make metal stronger and harder. They then used it to make better weapons.

Tribal Wars

During the Iron Age, tribes became larger and more powerful. They began to have kings or leaders. This was also the start of battles and wars between tribes. Life was harsh in the Iron Age, and there was a lot of **rivalry** between the tribes. Most of the hill forts in the British Isles were built during this time. Many hill forts were large enough for a whole village to live inside the protection of the **ramparts**. Some forts were so small that only one building could fit inside.

Why were hill forts built?

When we think of the word "fort" we often think of castles and battles. But **historians** believe that this is not the only reason hill forts were built.

Built for protection

Some hill forts were built just to protect the people inside from enemy attack. They had very tall **ramparts** and were built in a way that made them difficult to **invade**. Ramparts could be winding and maze-like, making them confusing to **invaders** trying to find a way in. Enemies trying to get past the ramparts were likely to be attacked by people up on the top throwing rocks or firing arrows down at them!

This photograph of the site of Maiden Castle shows that the defences were laid out like a maze.

Safe places

Hill forts were used for many different purposes, including storing food and farm animals. They were enclosed places where people could live safely together. The ramparts of a hill fort not only protected the people inside from invaders, but also from bad weather and wild animals. In the Iron Age the British Isles were home to wild animals, such as wolves and bears.

Special places

There are some hill forts that were far too small to be home to an entire tribe. Historians think that these might have been places built for **ceremonial** activities. Some historians even think that these forts were used as special places for their leaders, or just to show how powerful and important the tribe was. Historians believe that the fort at Mither Tap (below) was possibly used by a Pictish king in the late Iron Age.

Types of hill forts

There are many different types of hill forts. The type depends more on where the fort was built, than how it was built. Bronze and Iron Age people made use of the natural features of the land around them. Hill forts are mainly built on the very top of hills and are known as hilltop forts. They were built to follow the shape of the hill or the landscape. This means that they are all different shapes and sizes.

Defensive walls

Archaeologists often describe hill forts by the types of **defensive** walls they have. Univallate forts have one set of defensive walls, ditches and **ramparts**. Bivallate forts have two lots of defences. Multivallate have more than two defences.

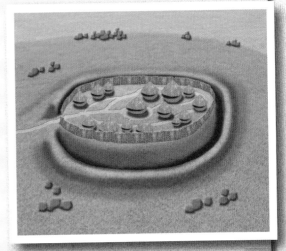

univallate fort

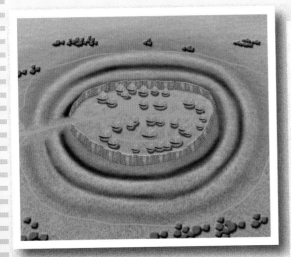

bivallate fort

multivallate fort

This photograph shows the site of an Iron Age fort at Dinas Gynfor. It lies on the north tip of Anglesey in Wales. Iron Age people built it on the edge of a cliff.

Good places to build hill forts

Some forts were built close to the sea. These forts use cliffs and rocks as part of the defensive building. Sea cliff forts are often built on rocky outcrops that only have a narrow stretch of land joining the fort to the mainland. This would make them easy to defend.

Some forts were built in an area where there were no high hills. These are called lowland hill forts. These made use of any ground that was a little higher, or on ground made higher by the people living there. They often have the largest ramparts and the deepest ditches. Some forts are built on dry land surrounded by marshes, or land that is difficult to cross on foot. There are even forts built at the bend of rivers, so the river water **meanders** around the fort.

How were hill forts built?

As we have seen, steep cliffs, rocky outcrops, rivers and the sea all helped to form natural defences against **invaders**. Hill forts were not built all in one go but were built over a long period of time. Most hill forts were added to over hundreds of years. One example of this is Maiden Castle in Dorset, England. **Archaeologists** believe people were constantly building Maiden Castle for over 300 years.

Building early hill forts

Early hill forts probably just had a simple wall built around the fort. The wall was made from stones and earth piled up, and then it was topped with wooden fences. This kind of **defensive** structure around a fort is called **fortification**.

This neat and tidy wall has survived since the late Iron Age, even though it has nothing to keep it stuck together.

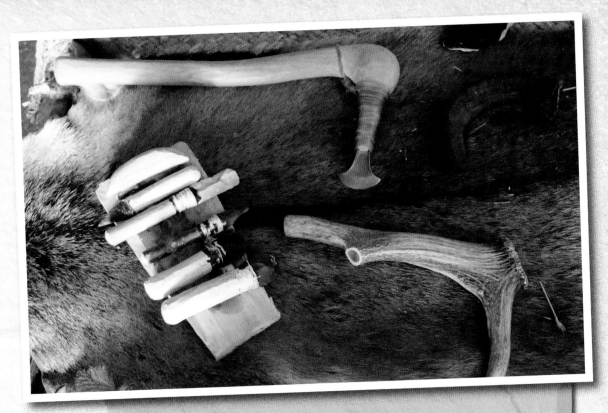

In the Bronze and Iron Ages, people used tools made of deer antlers, wood and stone, as well as metal.

Digging ditches

As hill forts became bigger and housed larger populations, people dug deep ditches around them for extra protection. Some ditches are over 7 metres (23 feet) deep. That is deep enough to stand a giraffe in and pat its head from the top!

Ramparts were then built above the ditches, and they towered high above them. Some ramparts almost doubled the full height of the fort to over 13 metres (43 feet). To build these forts, Bronze Age and Iron Age people would have had to move thousands of tonnes of rocks and soil.

Life in a hill fort

There was lots of **rivalry** between Iron Age tribes. This led to many battles. **Archaeologists** have found human remains with the scars of battle still on their bones. The high walls of a hill fort would have protected the tribe from their enemies, and from the worst of the winter weather.

Living together in one place would also have meant that people were able to share their food. This meant that people were less likely to go hungry during the winter. Outside the hill fort, the people farmed the land and grew wheat and barley. They also kept cattle, sheep and pigs.

These reconstructions show the kind of houses that people lived in during the Iron Age. You can visit these roundhouses at the Stonehenge visitor centre.

Houses

In the Iron Age, people lived in round buildings called roundhouses. These were made from wood. Plaster made from mud and chalk covered the walls. The roof was made of sticks that were tied together and covered with tightly packed straw. This type of straw roof is called a thatched roof. The whole family, often including grandparents, lived in one house together. The houses would have been dark inside and crowded, as they had no windows and only one room.

By the late Bronze Age and early Iron Age, people had become very skilled metalworkers. This necklace is made of very fine gold. It has been hammered out to a thin strip and then twisted. It was found in a burial mound in Scotland with 35 matching necklaces.

Work in a hill fort

Life inside a hill fort was busy, with traders and farmers coming and going all the time. In some hill forts archaeologists have found **evidence** of **metalworking**. They have also found weights from **looms**. This shows us that people were weaving cloth as well. So people not only lived in hill forts, but they worked and traded in them as well.

Other uses for hill forts

Not all hill forts were lived in all year round. Some were used only during the harvest time, when the tribes were gathering their crops. These forts had deep pits that were used as grain stores. Post holes have also been found. These show that the tribes built some very large buildings, much larger than the roundhouses. **Archaeologists** think that these might have been barns where animals and food were kept. These stores would have been used to feed the tribe through the long winter months.

This late Iron Age post hole still exists in Cornwall, England. The large posts that were the frame for the buildings would be wedged into the holes.

Romans

When the Romans **invaded** Britain in AD 43, they attacked and seized many hill forts, such as Old Sarum, below (see pages 22–23). The Romans often made the forts into **garrisons** for their soldiers. A large hill fort could hold many hundreds of Roman soldiers. They even built their roads right up to the forts to make travelling to and from them much easier.

War!

Some hill forts were only used when the tribe felt threatened and the people sheltered in the fort for safety. These forts had very large **defensive ramparts**. They would have had places that were used as watching points and **guardhouses**. Archaeologists have found the remains of weapons, such as rounded stones for handheld **slingshots**, shields, swords, axes, spears and arrows. Some of these forts had hidden entrances and exits to make them hard to get into. This also meant they would be easier to sneak out and run away from!

Maiden Castle

Maiden Castle in Dorset, England, is one of the largest Iron Age hill forts in Europe. It is so large that you could fit over 50 football pitches inside the **ramparts**! Maiden Castle was built around 500 BC and by 80 BC many hundreds of people were living inside the safety of the ramparts.

Maiden Castle had some of the tallest **fortifications** of all known hill forts. People would come and go through the wide entrance gates. In times of threat from other tribes, the gates would have been closed. The tribe would defend themselves from behind the huge ramparts.

Maiden Castle is a lowland hill fort. This means that it was built on flat land but raised up with high ramparts.

Life in the fort

Life in Maiden Castle would have been good most of the time. **Archaeologists** found **evidence** of large grain stores that could have stored enough food to feed everyone. There is also evidence of metalworkers making iron objects, and of other trades going on in the fort. For a long time, life would have been safe and people did not go hungry.

These ramparts are mostly built of chalk from the surrounding countryside. When they were first built, they would have been gleaming white and could be seen for miles.

Abandonment

Maiden Castle was lived in for many hundreds of years but, around 100 BC, people began to move away. **Historians** think that people left Maiden Castle to go and live in villages that were closer to their farmed fields. Some people remained in the fort. But around AD 43, the Romans attacked and seized Maiden Castle, and the last people **abandoned** life in the fort.

Danebury Hill Fort

Danebury Hill Fort in Hampshire, England, is one of the most **excavated** and studied hill forts in Europe. A lot of what we know about life in a hill fort comes from excavations at Danebury. There is **evidence** to suggest that around 300 people lived at Danebury in the Iron Age. The area has very few **natural resources**, such as tin and copper, and so the tribe would have had to trade with people in other areas to get these materials.

Danebury Hill Fort was first excavated in 1859 by Augustus Wollaston Franks (1826–1897). His workers found an Iron Age pit 2 metres deep but they could not work out what it was used for.

Building Danebury

Early in the Iron Age, the local tribe cleared trees from the highest hill in the area and built their fort on the top. Danebury Hill Fort was built around 600 BC, and was lived in for around 500 years. The fort had tall **ramparts** and a very large entrance gate. The entrance gate was hidden by **earthworks** and protected by a lookout point. From the lookout, the tribe could see their enemies coming. They would use **slingshot** stones and arrows to defend themselves.

Archaeologists found over 11,000 smooth stones in a pit at Danebury. The tribe would have used them as slingshot stones.

Life inside the fort

Inside the fort, **archaeologists** found evidence of very deep pits that would have been used to store grain. The many roundhouses inside the fort would have been built close to the walls. This would have protected them from the harsh winter weather. The central area of the hill fort was probably used for **ceremonial** occasions, and as a meeting place.

Old Sarum

The hill fort at Old Sarum in Wiltshire, England, was first lived on around 400 BC. This was during the late Iron Age. The fort is oval in shape and has two very deep ditches separated by tall banks. The Iron Age people carved out the natural slope of the hill to make it even steeper.

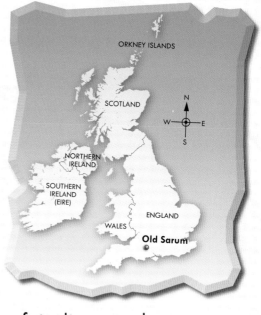

Historians think that Old Sarum was used as a marketplace and trading centre, as well as a place of safety. It covered a large area of over 12 hectares (29 acres), which is about the size of 20 football pitches! It could have protected a huge number of people in times of danger.

In some places, the height from the bottom of the ditch to the top of the **rampart** is over 13 metres (43 feet). That is deep enough to build a three-storey house in!

Roman camp

At the end of the Iron Age, the Romans took over the site and used it as a **military** camp. They renamed it Sorviodunum. Three Roman roads met outside the gates of the fort. Outside the walls of the fort, a large **settlement** began to grow. This settlement eventually became the city we know today as Salisbury.

Today you can visit the remains of a medieval cathedral at Old Sarum.

Many uses

Old Sarum is an unusual site because it was still in use right up to the 16th century. It started life as a **Neolithic** settlement, and then became a hill fort, a Roman camp, a Saxon stronghold, a medieval castle and the site of two cathedrals!

Tap O'Noth

Tap O'Noth is one of the highest hill forts in the British Isles. It is near Rhynie in Scotland and is on the top of a hill 563 metres (1,847 feet) high.

The tribe who lived at the hill fort would have had a clear view in all directions. From the top, they could see all the way to the sea, almost 50 kilometres (30 miles) away. The whole site is over 50 acres in size and would have been a safe place for a large tribe.

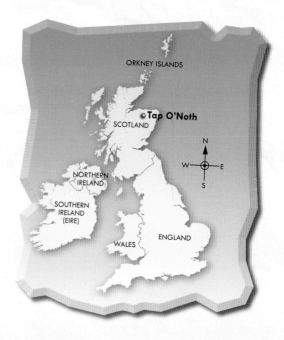

Rocks and stones are all that remain of the **ramparts** of Tap O'Noth. They can be seen easily from the base of the hill.

Archaeologists have found **evidence** of over 100 houses within the safety of the outer wall. Inside the walls, archaeologists have also found a deep hole that had been lined with stones. This was used to collect and store rainwater, as there was no fresh water nearby.

Melted stones!

The hill fort has a huge outer wall that was more than 6 metres (20 feet) wide and over 3 metres (10 feet) high. This wall was made of tonnes of stones that were piled up over wood and earth. The wall is very unusual because, in places, the stones have fused together. For the stones to melt in this way, they would have had to have been burnt for a long time in a massive fire. Archaeologists are not sure how this happened. Some think that the tribe set the stones on fire deliberately to make them stronger. Others think that the fort was attacked and burnt down, which caused the stones to melt together.

A great heat has melted these stones.
This is called **vitrification**.

Mither Tap

Mither Tap hill fort in Aberdeenshire, Scotland, is built on a rocky **crag** 518 metres (1,700 feet) high. Like Tap O'Noth, the hill is so high that it has a clear view in all directions.

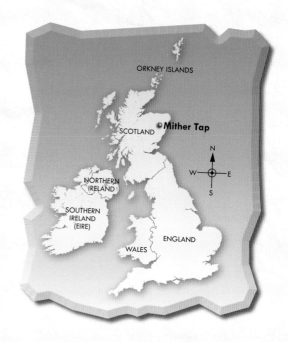

Some of the large stones found in the nearby stone circles were transported down from Mither Tap. The rocky top of the hill was used as the foundation, or solid base, for a large building that was inside a tall wall. At the foot of the building was a **terrace** with a few small roundhouses. **Archaeologists** think that the fort was first built earlier in the Iron Age, but that it was mainly used by a group of people called the **Picts**.

Through the remains of the ancient entrance at Mither Tap, you can see out across the landscape.

Mither Tap sticks up high above the forest around it. It can be seen from many miles away.

The Picts

The Picts were a tribal group of farmers. They lived in small **settlements** across Scotland during the late Iron Age. Like other Iron Age tribes, they began to make use of high ground and hill forts to keep their people safe during times of danger. They also used places like Mither Tap for **ceremonial** activities, and as places for their leaders to live.

Some **historians** believe that a Pictish king lived at Mither Tap sometime between AD 340 and AD 780. The fort is too small to hold a whole tribe, but it would have been a large and impressive building. Whoever lived at Mither Tap certainly wanted to show off how strong and powerful they were.

The Picts left many beautifully carved stones. This one from nearby shows a fish leaping over a porpoise.

Life for children in the Iron Age

We know that people used to play board games during the Iron Age. **Archaeologists** have found small gaming pieces at burial sites. Games would have been played using beads or small stones.

Life was mainly about hard work for children in the Iron Age. People then lived much shorter lives than we do today, so children had to grow up quickly. They spent most of their time learning skills that they would need to have when they were grown up. From a very young age, children learned how to look after animals, grow crops, weave cloth and bake bread. They were expected to do the same thing as their parents when they grew up.

Boys were also expected to become warriors, so on top of their other chores they would learn how to fight. Even very young boys would learn how to use a **slingshot**.

Bronze Age and Iron Age children were expected to help with many jobs in the home.